DREAMERS

MANOGYNA PODILA

Made with ❤ on the Notion Press Platform
www.notionpress.com

TO ALL THE UNCONQUERABLE SOULS

from your wonder_tara

Contents

Foreword   *xi*

Acknowledgements   *xiii*

Preface   *xv*

1. I'm A Poet   1

2. Mommy   3

3. Daddy   4

4. The Beautiful Me   5

5. India   6

6. My Shadow, My Path   8

7. The Aeroplane View   10

8. A Voodoo Doll   11

9. The Earth Is My Home   13

10. On The Way To School   14

11. Midnight Moonlight   16

12. I Am There For You   18

13. Little Things   20

14. Dreaming Be   22

15. The Best Poem   24

16. Neighbour   26

17. Being Invisible   28

18. Drought   29

19. Book   32

20. Time Travel   34

21. A Girl   35

Contents

22. Leaving Home — 37

23. Growing Older — 39

24. A Lovely Life Partner — 41

25. The Fateful Attempt — 43

26. At Midnight — 45

27. The Mild Oath — 46

28. Painful Lives — 48

29. The Hinder — 49

30. It Matters — 51

31. Let Me Tell Me — 53

32. Alone Dreams — 55

33. Sunrise — 56

34. There's Time — 57

35. A Dirty Move — 58

36. Catch It! — 60

37. Country Brutes — 61

38. Seasons Of Life — 63

39. Whats'up? Whats'app — 65

40. A Big Movement — 67

41. Nor The Girl I Be — 69

42. Those Memories — 71

43. Amity — 73

44. A Square Deal — 76

45. Granny's Home — 79

Contents

46. A Blind Belief   80

47. Pretty Girl   82

48. Seashore   84

49. Only You   85

50. Wild Friends Wild Dreams   87

51. Beach   89

52. Savitribai Phule   90

53. My Preacher   92

54. Michelle Obama   94

55. It's Life   95

56. My Tata   96

57. Noon   98

58. Helling Goal   99

59. Thoughts   101

60. Dejection   102

61. Pluto Case   104

62. Gardyloo   106

63. No One Elsewhere   107

64. Love   109

65. The Big-pocket   110

66. Traffic Jam   112

67. Big Hit   113

68. Colours   114

69. It's Me   116

Contents

70. A Haunted House   117

71. Morning   118

72. Fear   119

73. Evening   120

74. It Is You   121

75. Does It Happen   123

76. World Has To Bear It   125

77. Online Classes   126

78. Luck   127

79. Nature   128

80. Someone Good   129

81. Taking Leave   130

82. Politics   131

83. Old   132

84. Last Breadth   133

85. Marriage Anniversary   134

86. Birth And Death   136

87. Silly Mistakes   138

88. Our Tiny-tot   139

89. A Best Partner   141

90. Competing With Corona   143

91. धरती पुत्र   145

92. मेरी गुड़िया   147

93. कोरोना   148

Contents

94. लोखड़ौन ... 150

95. आई मेरी आई ... 152

96. दोस्त ... 153

97. जंगल ... 154

98. रीसेस ... 155

99. शक्षिक दविस ... 157

100. शब्द संपदा ... 158

Foreword

The first time when I held a pen in my hand, I was so much
obsessed with it.
I learnt that the pen is the tongue of the mind, and if you
want to change the world, pick up your pen and write!
And not so soon... I began to create something beautiful in the
meantime
and my happiness ever lies in writing with that pen I bought
when I was ten.
My whole career is sincerely dedicated to the strokes of pen
along with the beats of heart...
The way we dream depends on the thoughts we give !
And that's my motto.
Atlast, from the moment you give up on becoming yourself,
you will find what your inner me, the real you exactly wants.
I WALKED IN TO THE DEEP
AND WANT YOU TO BE THE HIDDEN ME
and then the life goes on....

Acknowledgements

Them that I love, know that I love them. This time I want to thank my readers, who have stuck with me through this whole epic roller coaster of the saga, through cliff-hangers and angst and feels.

I would specially thank my family members always for being with me and appreciating my art-work and creativity.

A heartfelt love and gratitude towards my parents, Dr. Pramod Chakravarthy and Mrs. Sree Usha.

A very very sweet regards to the troublesome heroes of my life, Mast. Arun and Mast. Hanuman.

A generous thanks to all the teachers, sisters, staff and my fellow classmates of Mount Carmel Girls' School, Nagpur who have guided me so far.

A sincere remembrance of all my buddies and sweethearts !!

Preface

This is my first time, i'm sharing my views as an author. And my preface goes like once upon a time in 2007

....

a star crashed the earth and took up a girly shape. Angels calls her Tara, while her parents call her Manu !

And that dear tara-manu grew up in a very very pleasant and peaceful atomsphere being the one and only princess of the family . Unless then in 2011 and 2013 respectively, two comets smashed the earth hitting on the star. Lo! that's so disgusting when you have two younger brothers .... and that's more likely an irritating thing in the world . But my brothers have the coolest sister of their own !!! I'm just saying!

And yes. My brothers are simply amazing and I just couldn't imagine my life without them; It would be great obviously !

An elder sister is like a brave father, caring mother, and a best friend all in one... admiringly that's me

The middle brother's always like a victim of older sibling, tormentor of younger sibling, somehow peace keeper between both of them.. unlike mine

Atlast the youngest brother is the hero of the family.... we can't ever describe him !

And gradually it's time for development :)

After long it's her 10th . God knows how ten years passed by so quickly while she grew up as a pretty little star in her school..

There came a time finally, when she lifted her pen with all her might

And the story continues....

1. I'm A Poet

I express my thoughts into words ,
with a glow on my face
and a beat on my heart ;
At the gentle cozy seat
beside the fire on sticks ,
wondering what next will be
when my maid brings me milk ,
in a mug hot to hold
till beyond my mind ,
I dream too big ;
From a dew on a daily
to the pot of ink ,
till a hail of summer
and the heat of spring ;
Through the truth and dare
I pen up beside ,
by the ages of life
I opt the pace of power ;
That time when sure of
a penny being paid ,
I never lay my wealth
down away to fade ;

I need a pen with ink and a book with pages ,
not a man with coat and a job with wages ;
The key of knowledge
and the jar of truth ,
are my little strengths
And I am a Poet !

- Manogyna Podila

Meanings :

1.   *Cozy - giving a feeling of comfort, warmth and relaxation.*
2.   *Dew - tiny drops of water that form on cool surfaces at night, when atmospheric vapour condenses.*
3.   *Wages - daily payment for work.*

2. Mommy

A lovely word which touches the heart is 'MOM'...
Mom, your arms spread vast
around me like an ocean ...
Your cheeks shine in pink
your little hug gives me energy
to do everything ...
And your pretty smile lets me forget
everything, but sleep on your lap ...
Mom, you are full of magic
which is known by none .
You are a lady full of patience,
your work is due without vacations .
I wonder, don't you get tired ?
that's the reason, why you are admired .
I love you Mom ...
I am your jerry,
you are my tom !

- Manogyna Podila

Meanings :

1.   *Admired - to respect or like somebody.*
2.   *Due - on time.*

3. Daddy

You are a man of incredible peace,
you are a teacher without taking fees.
You are a wonderful person i've ever met,
you are my owner, i'm your pet.
I wonder how can you manage everything with ease,
that was quite surprising, as hardworking as bees.
Tender, love and care, I get,
no one gets it easily, I bet.
Your affection towards me is unmatchable,
that is ever never stable,
which, I can express it as a fable.
I love you Dad …
I'm sorry for I make you sad,
one more opportunity, if I had,
i'll see to it, that you don't feel bad .

- Manogyna Podila

Meanings :

1. *Incredible - impossible or very difficult to believe.*
2. *Stable - steadily.*
3. *Fable - a short story.*

4. The Beautiful Me

I am a good girl
with some of the good qualities,
I love the people who are with me and will be.
I am strict with people who are wrong to me,
I listen to people who are good enough
and more experienced than me ;
At last, i'm a mixture of all the good manners
made by the Lord, the Almighty God !
And I am good enough and proud to say ...
that, I am a "Beautiful Me" !!

- Manogyna Podila

5. India

India, land of cultures ,
India, origin of rivers ;
India, famous for festivals ,
India, known for traditions ;
India, mother of religions ,
India, region of seven sisters ;
India, fame for mysterious wonders ,
India, pride of young brave-hearts ;
India, native of heavenly Gods ,
India, born to bring thoughts ;
India, sub-continent of Asia ,
India, third largest than Russia ;
India, population of billion ,
India, ready to serve alien ;
India, also named Hindustan ,
India, home for Registhan ;
India, shelter for twenty nine states ,
India, always there for team-mates ;
India, ever attracting tourists ,
India, ready to face blitz ;
India, always holy ,
India, brings glory !

- Manogyna Podila

Meanings :

1. *Mysterious - strange.*
2. *Alien - foreign.*
3. *Blitz - a sudden attack.*

6. My Shadow, My Path

My shadow follows me through
every corner of the town,
Through the hills and plains
through the driving rains.
Follows me through the darkness,
and discovers the light.
All through the stream,
with a gleam;
follows me on every path.
I didn't knew where had it been,
at night, when I dream.
At last I discovered that,
it is with me on every path ;
and always with me on every path.
It is a beam,
which can be seen;
all through the world,
following my path.

- Manogyna Podila

Meanings :

1. Stream - a small river.

2. *Gleam - a sudden expression of an emotion in somebody's eyes.*

3. *Beam - light.*

• 9 •

7. The Aeroplane View

Flying higher and higher,
as we see the world;
Hitting the clouds, touching the blows,
hearing the sound creep-creep-creep;
Enjoying the fresh blowing breeze.
One day I dreamt, I stepped on stars,
jumping from one to another;
I kept on dreaming, when I heard a call ;
Of beards chirping all around.
By the time, I woke up and looked around,
It was "a day";
When I heard the call.

- Manogyna Podila

8. A Voodoo Doll

I made a voodoo doll at night,
I kept it far off my sight;
I felt thirsty after a while,
I got up my bed to drink the nile.
At that midnight, I walked down the stairs,
I thought that there's no one who cares;
there was jet black where I walked,
it seemed that just now someone talked.
Then I quickly switched my torchlight,
that was efficient and reflected bright.
Just then turned around and saw,
the reflection of an inverted paw.
Then dropped the torchlight off my hand,
I just could not help to stand.
Just then appeared a little host,
that was none other than a ghost.
My body then trembled in fear,
and found a wall to adhere.
What that kind of ghost, I thought,
but quickly ran up to my cot.
I spread the bedsheet all around,
then thought, I need best profound,

to fight against that resound.
Next morning, I woke up late,
and walked down to test my fate,
reached the spot near the gate.
I then tried to look up and see,
was surprised and felt a bit free.
That was the voodoo doll, I made,
and hanged it over to stop it fade.
I thank, God the one who saved,
from the incident, which was engraved.

- Manogyna Podila

Meanings :

1. *Nile - a lagest river in the world.*
2. *Jet black - dark black.*
3. *Efficient - without mistakes.*
4. *Inverted - put upside down.*
5. *Trembled - shaked.*
6. *Adhere - to stick firmly.*
7. *Cot - a bed.*
8. *Profoud - needing a lot of knowledge.*
9. *Resound - an echo.*
10. *Fate - be destined to happen in a particular way.*
11. *Fade - lose colour.*
12. *Engraved - to be fixed in mind.*

9. The Earth Is My Home

The Earth is my home,

it is very well known;

I strive to keep it,

for years and more.

It is full of wonders, more than seven,

sound that wanders, is likely a heaven;

It is a place with scenic beauty,

also a place meaned to be mighty.

I love my home,

it is very well known;

I strive to keep it,

till I am no more !

- Manogyna Podila

Meanings :

1. *Strive - to try very hard to do or get something.*
2. *Mighty - very strong or powerful.*

10. On the Way to School

Daily when I go to school, I like to look afar,
I often feel the breeze that's cool, and try to see Bihar.
God has gifted me this morning,
when no one likes to wake up;
I hear the lovely birds are calling,
and have a little coffee cup.
I get ready by the sounds of clock,
and wait for the bus to arrive;
I admire the birds in flock,
and also a bee in hive.
On the way, I come across,
many a things left alone;
the heavenly shield with a boss,
so I think that I should own.
Birds are chirping all the way,
I can see the light-house glow;
butterflies can be seen to play,
and can also watch the flow.
Oh! how beautiful is the world in nature,
to have been ever special;
when always happy is the creature,
and is although casual.

By the time I reach my school,
having my mind searching somewhere;
where the nature seems to rule,
so I do much care!

- Manogyna Podila

Meanings :

1. *Hive - a bee hive.*
2. *Boss - a knob at the centre of the shield. (knob - a ball shaped handle)*
3. *Flow - a steady continuous stream.*

11. Midnight Moonlight

Come on boys and girls,
out of your little huts ;
Come hither, come hither, come hither ....
here is the moonlight ,
in this midnight;
Off your sight,
getting ready to shun;
loves to live in the sun.
This is the time to wake up,
and have a look at this breakup.
behind the clouds,
playing hide-and-seek;
in the dim light,
Sun and moon ready to fight.
Sleeping sun and waning moon,
are here for you tonight;
Oh come hither, come hither, come hither ....
and have a look at this midnight moonlight.

- Manogyna Podila

Meanings :

1. *Hither - come to or towards this place.*

2.   *Shun - avoid or reject.*

3.   *Waning - becoming smaller.*

12. I am There for You

Through the grief and sorrow,
through the dark and the dim;
through the deep and the hollow,
through the dull and the vim.
Through the rough and the tumble,
through the bob and the jiffy;
through the intone and the humble,
through the pride and the tiffy.
I am there for you, through the path you go,
I am there for you, through the way you show.
I am there for you, my loved ones,
though you are a little afar from me;
But i'm there for you, my worry proves,
that I think about none other than thee.
You may not make out,
for i'm always so silent;
But may remember me life-long,
as a saviour of you through the world violent.
I am there for you my little one,
for I am the cause of you;
I am there for you my child,
for I may suffer too...

- Manogyna Podila

Meanings :

1.   *Vim - energy, enthusiasm.*
2.   *Bob - a quick, short movement.*
3.   *Jiffy - a very short time, a moment.*

13. Little Things

The chunks of paper wood,
spreading all around here,
ebb into the nest,
where pretty little chicks bear.
The dust of earthy shoe,
cope up amazed like;
Why's stuff gathered around,
things prick as pike.
The gong of holy bell,
struck right at poles;
give away the way,
and hide through the holes.
Little things we hear,
play through the way;
ignite up the minds, of fresher's, I say!

- Manogyna Podila

Meanings :

1.   *Chunk - a thick solid piece of some thing.*
2.   *Ebb - move away.*
3.   *Cope - to deal with.*
4.   *Gong - resonant sound.*

5. *Ignite - to light up.*

14. Dreaming Be

We often dream the daily night,
could be knowing silly that might.
By the sleep on to head,
never last adventure bed.
Although facing busy lifetime,
also nursing deadly crime.
Thy ye stable whole night be,
coming across he or she.
Nor the mould be guy free,
setting the branches of fir tree.
Think why loiter I should be,
making nosh with a cup of tea.
Counting the stars that lay loll high,
wishing to fling and ever fly.
The ought of having mousy mooch,
but I warn you to catch the cooch.
World in dreams opt organic,
though having born in attic.
The great surmise knew no bounds,
leading the pitfall dismay to pounds.
Wondering spite giant alley,
Be the one to dream blind gay!

- Manogyna Podila

Meanings :

1.   *Thy - your.*
2.   *Ye - you.*
3.   *Nor - not.*
4.   *Mould - a distinctive style or character.*
5.   *Loiter - stand around idly.*
6.   *Nosh - food.*
7.   *Loll - hanging loosely.*
8.   *Fling - a short period of enjoyment.*
9.   *Ought - expressing probability.*
10.   *Mousy - timid.*
11.   *Mooch - pass time aimlessly.*
12.   *Opt - make a choice.*
13.   *Attic - a very small room inside a pointed roof.*
14.   *Surmise - suppose something is true.*
15.   *Knew-no-bounds - to have no limit.*
16.   *Pitfall - trap.*
17.   *Dismay - disappoint.*
18.   *Spite - deliberately annoyed or upset.*
19.   *Alley - a narrow passage between or behing buildings.*

15. The Best Poem

I write poems when I rest,
I get confused to choose the best.
Sun or moon or stars or sky,
Better to live near-by;
don't dare think to fly.
Poems are just thoughts of mine,
on mango, palm, neem, and pine.
Don't know to choose the best,
think and do if it is must;
don't get confused and let it dust.
Writer is a scientist,
his poems are inventions;
can a scientist choose his best invention?
that will be a big suspension.
Maybe TV, bulb, mobile, and rail,
are the hardworks that led him jail;
can he choose the best among all?
If he's confused he tries to call,
his friends and families and more to solve.
If one of them suggests one,
the other tells another;
will the scientist bother?

Same happens with the writer,
and gets to choose the other.
One or two or three or four,
try to expect more and more.
Never to settle only with one,
try to write on bread and bun;
It is a job to bring you fun!

- Manogyna Podila

Meanings :

1. *Invention - a thing that has been made or designed by somebody for the first time.*
2. *Suspension - delaying something for a period of time.*

16. Neighbour

My neighbour is so cozy,
My neighbour's likely crazy;
My neighbour gossip's buzzy,
My neighbour seems so whizzy.
My neighbour shows off cool,
My neighbour acts like fool;
My neighbour makes many a tool,
My neighbour does never pool.
My neighbour signs so high,
My neighbour does always sigh;
My neighbour's ever guy,
My neighbour's likely die;
I like to say good-bye!
(note: here die refers to be very eager for or to do)

- Manogyna Podila

Meanings :

1.   *Crazy - very foolish or mad.*
2.   *Gossip - casual or unconstrained conversation or reports about other people, typically involving details that are not confirmed as being true.*
3.   *Buzzy - a low continuous sound.*

4.   *Whizzy - move or go fast.*

5.   *Cool - fashionly attractive and unfriendly.*

6.   *Fool - act in a joking or silly way.*

7.   *Pool - share.*

8.   *Signs - an indication that something exists, is occuring or may occur.*

9.   *High - large in amount, value and size and cannot be controlled by anybody.*

10.   *Sigh - expressing sadness.*

11.   *Die - be very eager for or to do.*

17. Being Invisible

I like to be invisible,
when caught of teacher's hand;
I like to be invisible,
and rule over the land.
I like to be invisible,
when mom calls to work;
I like to be invisible,
and disappear suddenly with a jerk.
I like to be invisible,
when I and you together play;
I like to be invisible,
and speed up to bay.
I like to be invisible,
when stuck in a traffic jam;
I like to be invisible,
when people wonder where I am!

- Manogyna Podila

Meanings :

1. *Jerk - a sharp, sudden movement.*
2. *Bay - seashore.*

18. Drought

Drought forby husbandman smite ,
nay love apple , nay raiment , nay meat .
Nary pismire , popinjay , grimalkin steed ,
venery wannion ware peradventure speed .
Sable recreant whenas esurient estate ,
morrow methinks malison glaciate .
Orison quoth sore enow foresooth fore ,
erewhile at fane fair fandangle overbrim ere .
Pore on prithee parfay Oo! puissant ,
sith thenceforth saturnism swith for aliment .
Maugre leech , man-at-arms marry gyve ,
lucifer , lief , larcener , lurdan , knave .
Ruth on the quick sanative slugabed ,
baseborn athwart appetency forefend .
Grateful , gorgonize greenwood guerdon ,
heyday groaks kickshaw hereupon .

- Manogyna Podila

Meanings :

1.   *Drought - thirst.*
2.   *Forby - past, near.*
3.   *Husbandman - farmer.*

4.   *Smite - defeat or conquer.*

5.   *Nay - no.*

6.   *Loveapple - tomato.*

7.   *Raiment - clothing.*

8.   *Meat - any kind of food.*

9.   *Nary - not at all.*

10.   *Pismire - ant.*

11.   *Popinjay - parrot.*

12.   *Grimalkin - cat.*

13.   *Steed - horse.*

14.   *Venery - hunting.*

15.   *Wannion - ill luck, misfortune.*

16.   *Ware - aware of.*

17.   *Peradventure - perhaps.*

18.   *Speed - Prosperity.*

19.   *Sable - black mourning clothes.*

20.   *Recreant - cowardly.*

21.   *Whenas - when.*

22.   *Esurient - hungry.*

23.   *Estate - condition in life, period.*

24.   *Morrow - the folloing day.*

25.   *Methinks - it seems to me.*

26.   *Malison - a curse.*

27.   *Glaciate - freeze over.*

28.   *Orison - a prayer.*

29.   *Quoth - said.*

30.   *Sore - extremely.*

31.   *Enow - enough.*

32.   *Foresooth - in truth, indeed.*

33.   *Fore - at an early time or period.*

34.   *Erewhile - until now.*

35.   *Fane - shrine or temple.*

36.   *Fair - beautiful.*

37.   *Fandangle - a useless or pureles ornamental thing.*

38.   *Overbrim - spill, overflow.*

39.   *Ere - before.*

40.   *Pore on - think about.*

41.   *Prithee - expression of wish or request.*

42.   *Parfay - by my faith.*

43.   *Puissant - mighty or powerful.*

44.   *Sith - since.*

45.   *Thenceforth - from that time, place or point onward.*

46.   *Saturnism - lead poisioning.*

47.   *Swith - instantly.*

48.   *Aliment - food, nourishment.*

49.   *Maugre - in spite of.*

50.   *leech - a doctor or healer.*

19. Book

I am a book,
quickly have a look;
I am neat,
till i'm covered with a sheet.
I am happy when you take me home,
I feel sad when you leave me;
and look for chrome.
I get pain when you tear my pages,
and scribble on me;
I get upset and think about thee,
where there's no one to see.
I give you knowledge about the world,
I make your name around unfurled.
Without me, no one is there,
so protect me, share and care.
Remove darkness from your mind,
path to success that you'll find.
I am the god of wisdom and grace,
people all, the dreams they chase;
respect me so that you can face,
all the troubles and then get to race;
for all the days...

In this case,
the person who says;
"Books are mirrors",
and always prays;
there's no one ever to chase.

- Manogyna Podila

Meanings :

1. *Scribble - to make marks with a pen or pencil and write something quickly and carelessly.*
2. *Thee - you.*
3. *Unfurled - spread out.*

20. Time Travel

Travel travel to and fro,
travel makes you never bore.
Up to the mountains, over the hills,
time to enjoy and have thrills.
Under the ground, hover round,
time to move and readily bound.
Upto the height, all the night,
time to wonder and have a bite.
Travel makes a man unfurl,
travel bakes the time you whirl.
Travel lays the man in peace,
travel bays the success bearing keys.
Travel travel to and fro,
time to travel, where you know.

- Manogyna Podila

Meanings :

1. *Thrills - a sudden strong feeling of pleasure or excitement.*
2. *Hover - to stay in the air in one place.*
3. *Bound - certain to do something.*
4. *Unfurl - spread out.*
5. *Whirl - a state of confusion or excitement.*

21. A Girl

Once she was happy, to be a girl
but not so far till now,
By the hardships, she has faced
accepted the life with bow.
No matter what the others think of her
she went on along the way,
Never gave up life on behalf of oneself's slave
but carried the hope each day.
With equal determination and faith
stood up firmly like a tree,
Thought of someone above
who might let her free.
Days passed and years went on
as she grew up old,
Would admire her for she never complained
the life bitter to hold.
With patience to bring her springs right now
she worked hard to feed,
Overcoming remarks put up on her
she payed the mother-hood seed.
Gaining age, right so high
when children left her all alone,

She was suffering, behind the bars
in her was sadness sown.
Waiting for them, at the doors
forgot to eat and drink to live,
After long when her grief knew no bounds
she thought her life to give.
A girl's life forever's the same
as we people pay no attention to them,
What we think is, they're no use to us
it's none other than mankind's shame.
What a woman does for each of us
we haven't yet known,
For she's always there, by our side
we've reached this height and grown.
So lets pray tribute to our female friends
who lay their lives apart,
For these ruthless creatures, on earth
lets salute them, from heart !

- Manogyna Podila

Meanings :

1. *Slave - a person who is the legal property of another and is forced to obey them.*
2. *Springs - (offsprings) children of own.*
3. *Knew no bounds - have no limits.*
4. *Ruthless - having or showing no pity or compassion for others.*

22. Leaving Home

I love my home
I wondered if I were a gnome,
And travelled across with the help of chrome
Also the places filled with foam;
I would be strong enough to roam
The whole world including Rome,
And saw the sculpture of great Bome
That was although kome;
And rested in a hut which was dome
And soon after the gloam,
Flew off by the drome
Landed late on the bay of loam;
And met a passerby mome
Who gave me an old tome,
I read that tome and found out loam
Very soon, I grew the pome;
And thought, I had my vome
At last I felt, I missed my home,
Which was the best among the gome.

- Manogyna Podila

Meanings :

1.   Gnome - a little old man with a beard and a pointed hat who lives underground.

2.   Foam - a mass of small air bubbles that form on surface of a liquid.

3.   Roam - walk or travel.

4.   Bome - the pseudonym (pen name) of a Japanese sculptor.

5.   Kome - rare.

6.   Dome - spherical in shape.

7.   Gloam - the time immediately following sunset.

8.   Drome - an aerodrome.

9.   Lome - capital and largest city of Togo, located in the south on the gulf of gunea.

10.   Mome - a dull, silent person.

11.   Tome - a large heavy, scholarly book.

12.   Loam - good quality soil, containing sand, clay and dead plants.

13.   Pome - a fruit consisting of a fleshy enlarged reseptacle and a tough central core containing the seeds.

14.   Vome - victory over many enemies.

15.   Gome - a fighter or combatant who engages in battle.

23. Growing Older

I was as small as a bottle guard, when I was born,
my mother towards me would be very fawn;
No. 1 when I aged,
I was protected and was caged;
Two and three when I crossed,
put in school, slowly paused,
for a while and then bossed;
Growing up was so fun,
that was the thing I thought,
but very soon I was caught;
I just knew that gaining height and weight was enough,
for growing up and becoming tough;
The day when I passed thirteen,
I felt that my freedom was certain;
Today I feel like,
I experienced a deep hike;
I didn't like growing old,
I think I should put a hold;
I even thought, why did I grew up,
being small was as better as not stoking up.

- Manogyna Podila

Meanings :

1.   *Fawn - very attentive.*
2.   *Tough - strong enough to withstand wear and tear.*
3.   *Hike - a sharp increase.*
4.   *Stoking - to make any emotion or conflict more violent.*

24. A Lovely Life Partner

A lovely life partner is the one,
with whom we have to share the fun;
Not that one is superior and the other inferior,
those are only in one's minds,
that's not of people's kind;
All are equal for the children,
never be a strike for the woman;
One may be rich, one may be poor,
one may be high, one may be low;
one may be beautiful, and the other ugly,
but their hearts should join each other.
There's no home without a fight,
where there's fight, there is love;
misunderstanding till the height,
there should be one ready to bow.
Problems are just small injections,
with each one's specifications;
without having proper supervisions.
A lovely life partner is the one,
who bows to the other and thinks to shun;
Not with frustrations as many,
with their minds thinking cunny.

Choose your life partner with a brain,
not to use it up like a grain;
One fight, the other surrender,
if this might, i'll remember;
for november and december...

- Manogyna Podila

Meanings :

1. *Superior - a person of high position.*
2. *Inferior - a person with low position.*
3. *Srike - harm.*
4. *Frustration - feeling of anger.*

25. The Fateful Attempt

Though beef-witted , my life got shattered ,
It was the third time ;
I built bricks upon my brains ....
Away since they gathered ,
My dame gave me dreams ;
upon flames....
Expiry be their vision ,
Completion be my mission ;
Beautiful is my passion ,
insane....
Forward i'd to deal with ,
Merry be my patience ;
That one freaks up my whim ,
sustained....
Zigzag got my glowing ,
Flowers led me showing ;
Fateful got up screaming ,
Now i'd to end the feeling....

- Manogyna Podila

Meanings :

1. *Freak - a very unusual and unexpected event or situation.*

2. *Whim - a sudden desire or change of mind, especially one that is unusual and unexplained.*

3. *Sustained - continuing for an extended period or without interruption.*

26. At Midnight

At the midnight, on the stairs
when the clock rang twelve,
it was dark by our lane
where there was alone myself.
Haunting ghosts passing by,
frequent grunts made by caves;
where restless dogs moving on,
chasing for their winter prays.
There was silence until on,
till then I walked bare foot;
suddenly at last, when I passed,
my boot on the helpless goat.
My body started to shiver,
at that terrible night I know;
passed from scary woods so far,
finally reached my home.

- Manogyna Podila

Meanings :

1.   Grunts - a low, short guttural sound made by animals.

27. The Mild Oath

Thee loveth best,
the savage crew;
Thy hose of reef,
is dark like few.
The kegs of blood,
in the soul of veins;
At the foot of sake,
will hit the holds pains.
The ribs of bark,
in a wink of tide;
May fly the smoke,
with grims to hide.
More the might,
the more the shore;
In the tear of tear,
onto the core.

- Manogyna Podila

Meanings :

1. *Thee - you.*
2. *Loveth - to love.*
3. *Crew - a group of people who work closely together.*

4. *Thy - your.*

5. *Hose - a flexible tube.*

6. *Reef - below the surface of the earth.*

7. *Kegs - underpants.*

8. *Wink - a shine or flash.*

9. *Grims - fierce in disposition or action.*

28. Painful Lives

Little pains of darkness,
little pains so rude;
little pains of sadness,
make the pains so good.
Little pains of hardships,
little pains so many;
little pains of turn-points,
make the pains of journey.
Little pains of sorrow,
little pains of rife;
little pains of grief,
make the pains of life.

- Manogyna Podila

Meanings :

1. *Rife - (especially of something undesirable) of common occurrence; widespread.*

29. The Hinder

The carriage carried my clothes,
when I was left behind;
The bars closed by me,
it seemed, I could never find.
Though hastily ....
the clock ran out fuel;
As busy as a bee,
my soul caught to drool.
In vain conceited drive,
modest be my wife;
A clew and a clout I carried away.
Compeer by bloody veins,
regarding with the sails;
All gone away ....
Meanwhile we took a stand,
above the silly death note;
We named it the suicide squad,
in truth feels the bored.
A buss in a mood,
helped them withstand;
Hence gave upon,
their heavenly shrines.

- Manogyna Podila

Meanings :

1.   *Hinder - make it difficult for (someone) to do something or for (something) to happen.*
2.   *Hastily - with excessive speed or urgency ; hurriedly.*
3.   *Drool - drop saliva uncontrollably from the mouth.*
4.   *Vain - producing no result ; useless.*
5.   *Conceited - excessively proud of oneself ; vain.*
6.   *Modest - unassuming the estimation of one's abilities or achievements.*
7.   *Clew - a ball of thread.*
8.   *Clout - a piece of cloth or clothing.*
9.   *Compeer - a companion or company ; close associate.*
10. *Buss - a kiss.*

30. It Matters

It matters for the dawn and dusk,
it matters for the boor;
It matters for the tooth and tusk,
it matters for the poor.
It matters for the coy and crave,
it matters for the foolish;
It matters for the bold and brave,
it matters for the amateurish.
It matters for the bright and dim,
it matters for the grim;
It matters for the foe and fawn,
it matters for the Amazon.
It matters for the deer and lion,
it matters for the alstain;
It matters for the pebble and crystal,
it matters for the apostle.
It matters for the core and crust,
it matters for the lust;
It happens only just !
It matters for the people who think,
about it again and again;
Who lay, peace of mind beside,

and walk in the path of pain.

- Manogyna Podila

Meanings :

1. *Boor - a rough and bad mannered person.*
2. *Amateurish - done in an unskilful or inept way.*
3. *Alstain - a dog breed.*
4. *Apostle - an important christian teacher.*

31. Let Me Tell Me

Oh! my mind blows hard
Oh! the time goes pale
Oh! for the flowers that bloom
Oh! that the chill gets soon
For all, tell me, tell me...
My soul, let me, let me...
Those eyes caught me, caught me
My flames get me, get me
My heart bit me, bit me
My life fit me, fit me
C'mon, tell me, tell me
My soul let me, let me
For he saw me, saw me
And lol! kick me, kick me
For all tell me, tell me
My soul let me, let me
Oh! my, lit me, lit me
Oh! peace, hit me, hit me
Oh! please, get me, get me
With you, fill me, fill me
That's cool, pick me, pick me
Oh! God, catch me, catch me

As me, am the me-me....

- Manogyna Podila

Meanings :

1. *Pale - seem or became less important.*

32. Alone Dreams

I am alone, all alone,
I don't have a single backbone;
Worries, tensions, sadness and more,
I don't know when will it cure?
I don't know anyone is alone,
like me without a bone;
Support is needed for all the ones',
courage is needed to fight for the guts.
Help the one's who are alone,
bring the support to stand by own;
Love them and care for them,
and listen to their feelings;
Co-operate with them,
unless it's a boon to them...!

- Manogyna Podila

Meanings :

1.   Guts - enough courage, conviction.
2.   Boon - a thing that is very helpful and that you are grateful
for.

33. Sunrise

Sunrise meant to be so pleasant,
Sunrise caught to have sweet scent.
Sunrise made to wake up bright,
Sunrise laid foundation to light.
Sunrise seems fluoroscent,
Sunrise always symbolizes gent.
Sunrise makes the affection warm,
Sunrise flees the evil, calm.
Sunrise signs many a values,
Sunrise glows from pile to plateus.

- Manogyna Podila

Meanings :

1. *Scent - sweet smell.*
2. *Fluoroscent - giving out bright light when exposed to radiation such as UV rays.*
3. *Gent - gentle.*
4. *Flees - run away from a place or situation of danger.*
5. *Signs - is a sign of.*
6. *Pile - a large amount.*
7. *Plateus - an area of level above the ground.*

34. There's Time

There's time to do everything,
it's time for everything;
There's time for the things we do,
it's time to do;
There's time for the dawn and dusk,
it's time for the dusk;
There's time for sun and moon,
it's time for the moon;
There's time for birth and death,
it's time to cope for death;
There's time for one and all,
it's time for all;
There's time for you and me,
now it's the time of me!

- Manogyna Podila

Meanings :

1. *Dawn - the first appearance of light in the sky before sunrise.*
2. *Dusk - the darker stage of the twilight.*

35. A Dirty Move

Haha, we toiled hard,
haha, it showed no bad.
Haha, it wasn't free,
haha, it couldn't pee.
Haha, maybe it grows,
haha, but won't make shows.
Haha, we weren't shamed,
haha, it could be tamed.
Haha, we made much more,
haha, we studied the core.
Haha, it showed some signs,
haha, then manisha resigns.
Haha, that was the past,
haha, which was fast and vast.
Haha, much higher it costs,
haha, it was never lost.

- Manogyna Podila

Meanings :

1. *Toiled - work extemely hard or incessantly.*
2. *Tamed - to control or domesticate.*

3. Core - the part of something that is central to its existence or character.

4. Resign - voluntarily leave a job or office.

5. Vast - of great extent ; immense.

36. Catch It!

Go, go, go ahead!
try not only sit on bed;
There's more to do, sleepy head,
more and more till the little lives shed.
Go, go, go alone!
wake up early to rise your tone,
Early and early till success you own,
for your name to be world known.
Go, go, go turned blind!
will surely catch the path you find,
Surely and surely will overcome the bind;
you'll catch it and be named the shined!

- Manogyna Podila

Meanings :

1. Bind - a difficult situation.

37. Country Brutes

It was a mare

at night I got,

for a very few days

I could never stop.

My mind away

was hit by shot,

and soon always

they're hid in a pot.

And la-di-loo-loo-hoo!

For I always

say strange things alone,

and they get up

to be the best known,

Oh! fire under miles

our seeds were sown.

And la-di-loo-loo-hoo!

We broke up things

we broke up tools,

we had no baths

nor jumped in the pools.

We danced and sang

and were named country brutes...

And laa-di-loo-loo-hoo!

- Manogyna Podila

Meanings :

1. *Mare - a very unpleasant or frustrating experience.*
2. *Brute - a savagely violent person or animal.*

38. Seasons of Life

Migratory birds return
the sun shines brighter than before
many trees blossom,
humidity in the air increases
that's all for summer.
We see fog in the morning
nights become longer and the days shorter
there may sometimes be hail,
or snow in some places
humidity in the air decreases
that's all for winter.
New grass sprouts
tender leaves shoot out on plants and trees
there are sudden showers or hailstorms,
there is fresh smell of wet earth
Oh lo! that's the monsoon.
But oh! children are waiting
to get a play and dream,
of the little huge memories
of the school day chuttis.

- Manogyna Podila

Meanings :

1. *Migratory - moving from one place to another.*
2. *Blossom - produce flowers or masses of flowers.*
3. *Humidity - atmospheric moisture.*
4. *Fog - a thick cloud of tiny water droplets suspended in the atmosphere.*
5. *Hail - pellets of frozen rain which fall in showers from cumulonimbus clouds.*
6. *Snow - atmospheric water vapour frozen into ice crystals and falling in light white flakes or lying on the ground as a white layer.*
7. *Sprout - put out shoots.*
8. *Tender - gentle, kind.*
9. *Chuttis - holidays (in hindi).*

39. Whats'up? Whats'app

Say good morning, say good evening;
Say good night, switch off the light.
Each and every hour, say hello!
Just think what that kind of fellow.
Hello! Hi! day pass by...
At last you're a lonely guy.
Morning dew, shot a pic;
Peacock flew, again click.
Not a single moment, we live by;
There's never rest, for wi-fi.
There is not a use of single coin,
We too ask our friends to join.
Make groups and chat online,
Do always bother , "are you fine?"
Seeking for status, all the day;
Please leave that and go for play.
Hey Whats'app, what is up?
Dare not say that, God is up.
There's no phone wihtout you,
On you there's to be put a curfew.

You whas'app, please go-go-go;
Hey Almighty, help them know!

- Manogyna Podila

40. A Big Movement

If you wanna strive your goal,
it is necessary to feed your soul.
Make a movement known so big,
until you reach it, just dig-dig-dig.
The best possible way is by hardwork and pains,
do it for you may beg on lanes.
The sunlight gave you this morning to work,
get up early to make a big jerk.
God is the ultimate, so do pray day,
then the path you get, is the success way.
Nobody is there for you, through the dim and the dull,
just remember this and move on to shall.
You'll have no one just beside you, by the truth and dare,
so leave the relations and the people you care.
Try to be the hero to your little living,
Stick to your hopes, for you're nowhere in dreaming.
So make a movement known so big,
until you reach it, just dig-dig-dig!

- Manogyna Podila

Meanings :

1. Jerk - a quick, sharp, and sudden movement.

2.   *Dim - not shining brightly or clearly.*

41. Nor the Girl I be

As a tender tinklin' wild and glow ,
Envy that maiden with silken robes ;
With a countless patches on my rags ,
Like autumn , my mind got free from nags .
In clad of the gentle dream maybe ,
For the flowers & the birds & the nests I be ;
In wander like sway for the gentle unseen ,
Left my buddy to be with me .
The stars with a wrath underneath ,
Gave me a cold & grey & bold like blow ;
For the moonlight , proud , I always be ,
And got my story untold .
Killed by the gaze of the wicked old piles ,
Hopes to the wonder , as far as I see ;
With the little pretty bewitching smiles ,
Nor the girl I be !

- Manogyna Podila

Meanings :

1. *Tender - showing gentleness, kindness, and affection.*
2. *Tinklin' - (tinkling) make or cause to make a light, clear ringing sound.*

3. *Envy - desire to have a quality, possession, or other desirable thing belonging to someone else.*

4. *Maiden - an unmarried girl or young woman.*

5. *Robes - a long, losse outher garment reaching to the ankles.*

6. *Rags - a piece of old cloth, especially one torn from a larger piece.*

7. *Nags - harass someone constantly to do something that they are averse to.*

8. *Clad - dressed or covered in.*

9. *Sway - move or cause to me slowly or rhythmically backwards or forwards or from side to side.*

10. *Buddy - a close friend.*

11. *Wrath - strong, fierce, extreme anger.*

12. *Gaze - a steady intent look especially in admiration, surprise, or thought.*

13. *Bewitching - enchanting or delightful.*

42. Those Memories

Those days when I was small,
my mother would be always with me;
Those nights when I would crawl,
my father would pick me up with glee.
Those hours which I had passed,
went on behind, where I had chased;
Those parks where I had played,
when monkeys jumped and the donkeys gazed.
Those trees which I had loved,
could seem to me always so great;
Those fruits which I had hate,
would be my present breakfast late.
Those toys with which i'd played,
would be so light in weight;
Those friends with whom i'd ever fight,
are now away at sight.
Those streets where I had fun,
at last nowhere to share the bun;
Those years when I used the slate,
is unforgettable and out of gate.
Those months for which i'd worry,
would not let my mother make curry;

Those weeks when i'd painted the walls,
had led my father more in calls.
Those times when i'd watch the meadows,
would leave me alone to catch the shadows;
Those lives for which i'd waited,
have passed so earlier, without being tasted.

- Manogyna Podila

Meanings :

1. *Meadows - a piece of grassland.*

43. Amity

She asked for money ,
But we haven't any ;
Tears filled in her eyne ,
It proved she wasn't fine .
The reason for alack , I asked her betwixt ,
Iwis I shall say , in sooth i'll hist .
Ilke the girl , I thought not jade ,
Will clepe the forward feminal , we'll cannonade .
Grateful the little damsel , to me she hight ,
Hither I should go , hence hie to fight .
Ifsoever I meet , thee all anent ,
Aught important anon , so i'm avaunt .
'Aye' I behold , thy path certes ,
But be with us , all ever betimes .
Eke eftsoons ere , you're here ,
We'll enjoy the apricity and fare .
Take this doit dight along for you ,
As far as you , nigh reach your shoe .
Bethink of our past , collogue , delate ,
For a fair goody , enow we wait !

- Manogyna Podila

Meanings :

1. *Amity - friendly relations.*
2. *Eyne - eyes.*
3. *Alack - expression of sorrow or regret.*
4. *Betwixt - between.*
5. *Iwis - surely; certainly.*
6. *In sooth - actually.*
7. *Hist - expression used to attract attention.*
8. *Ilke - kind in nature.*
9. *Jade - a bad-tempered or disreputable woman.*
10. *Clepe - to name.*
11. *Feminal - feminine, womanly.*
12. *Cannonade - bombard.*
13. *Damsel - a yound unmarried woman.*
14. *Hight - called.*
15. *Hither - to or towards this place.*
16. *Hence - from here.*
17. *Hie - go quickly.*
18. *Ifsoever - if ever.*
19. *Thee - you.*
20. *Anent - about; concerning.*
21. *Aught - anything at all.*
22. *Anon - at once; immediately.*
23. *Avaunt - away.*
24. *Aye - yes.*
25. *Behold - see or observe.*
26. *Thy - your.*
27. *Certes - in truth.*

28.   *Betimes - in short time; speedily.*

29.   *Eke - in addition; also; likewise.*

30.   *Ere - before.*

31.   *Apricity - a cold winter day with a warm sun.*

32.   *Doit - a very small amount of money.*

33.   *Dight - clothed or equipped.*

34.   *Nigh - nearly, almost.*

35.   *Bethink - oneseelf to remember; recollect.*

36.   *Collogue - talk confidently.*

37.   *Delate - report.*

38.   *Fair - beautiful.*

39.   *Goody - an elderly woman of humble position.*

40.   *Enow - enough.*

44. A Square Deal

Am I busy so much?

so much that i'm not leaving a moment?

To get into this nature,

and feel the beauty of things around me?

To understand the essence of life,

and find where pure happiness persists;

What have I done in my past?

and am doing in my present?

just finding me in the world of pain,

with misery where people all groan;

to wail, to weep, to sob, to grieve,

to cry, to mourn, to get the seed when sown.

I deplore on some when,

without a reason, they impel;

and how the courage,

of a cold feet fell.

When the hell and heaven got a hinge,

a dream heinous till the dawn lasts;

what we saw was not true ,

and what we heard was not ocular.

A claimant, a fraud, a humbug, an imposter,

I preclude, I impede, I avert, I restrain;

the world moves faster and things gape up around.
My obvious world left me alone,
and crushed me between eyes and nose.
Lament I, futile and in vain,
left me halp and weak and cripple and lame.
With a hasty conclsion, a prejudgement, a view,
tells me to get to an incite;
where I get to know a mow of the mean,
and get this life, a carte unseen.

- Manogyna Podila

Meanings :

1. *Square-deal - justice.*
2. *Misery - a state of feeling of great physical or mental distess or discomfort.*
3. *Groan - make a deep sound conveying pain, despair.*
4. *Deplore - feel or express strong disapproval of.*
5. *Cold feet - loss or lack of courage or confidence.*
6. *Hinge - a joint or connection.*
7. *Heinous - utterly odious or wicked.*
8. *Ocular - connected with eyes or vision.*
9. *Claimant - one who claims for something.*
10. *Humbug - a person who is a fraud or imposter.*
11. *Preclude - prevent from happening.*
12. *Impede - delay or prevent.*
13. *Avert - turn away or prevent.*
14. *Lament - expressing grief.*

15. *Futile - incapable of producing any useful result.*

16. *Prejudgement - a judgement reached before the evidence is available.*

17. *Incite - urge to make a quick decision.*

45. Granny's Home

Grandma , grandma , I'll stay with you ,
With you I be joyful and happy too .
Grandma , grandma , I'll not go to my house ,
Instead , I'll be with you and your spouse .
Grandma , grandma , always open doors for me ,
I'm big enough to take care of thee .
Grandma , grandma , I'll feed you well ,
To me all fables , you will tell .
Grandma , grandma , I'll gift you a new pair ,
Then you'll have to comb my hair .
Grandma , grandma , I'll complete the chores ,
To you anything , I'll not force .
Grandma , grandma , I'll do no late ,
Then I will come , and change your fate .
Grandma , grandma , I may be nine ,
But with me ever , you'll be fine .
Grandma , grandma , I love you ,
You are the only one , in a few !

- Manogyna Podila

Meanings :

1. *Chores - a routine task, especially a household one.*

46. A Blind Belief

A barren hit the peak of alive ,
And jostled by the siege ;
From eye to eye …
The weeping dragged the cold grey blews ,
And once they ate the nails and screws …
The frozen haunts of gallants and brave ,
For the host they believed ;
Somebody could save …
An elope with the past ,
For the deeds of the torn ;
By the epics of the the father ,
And the son unborn .
Fateful rejoice for the night untamed ,
Left behind , huge tales & tales ;
And so came out of leaping flames ,
A wonder to all , they could praise !

- Manogyna Podila

Meanings :

1. *Barren - too poor to produce much or any vegetation ; (of a place) bleak and lifeless.*
2. *Jostled - struggle or compete forcefully for.*

3.   *Siege - a persistent or serious attack.*
4.   *Gallants - dashing gentlemen.*
5.   *Elope - run away secretly.*

47. Pretty Girl

Once there was a girl,
who worked in a hotel;
she was just nine,
and the situation was fatal.
With her little arms,
she cleaned the dining tables;
and would pick up the tips;
from healthy wealthy nobles.
She would impress the guests,
by her little rich smiles;
and worked hard she could,
from the tops to tiles.
She would cook and clean,
all the plates and pans;
and would serve all well,
has all stomach-full fans.
I liked her dedication and simplicity,
loved her character and belongingness;
and asked her won't you come with me,
why work in this mess?
She replied with a sigh,
God gave me all I need;

i'm happy here to work,
i'll have to repay and feed.
Tears filled in my eyes,
her words touched my heart;
nothing I could say,
and I left her apart.

- Manogyna Podila

Meanings :

1. *Fatal - deadly.*

48. Seashore

A bay visible from my window door ,
Is a giant and large and a huge seashore.
With its little pretty golden sand ,
It brightens up the entire land .
The sun rays falling off below ,
Give my sea a holy glow.
Besides breezy busy broad day light ,
I love the cozy colourful night .
It entertains the exhausted visitors ahead ,
And lits up their faces by the seashore bed .
The warm hug that waters give ,
In our healthy heart the memories live .
That big lighthouse which stands alone ,
Shoos darkness and the path is shown .
The trees , the birds , the people are fond ,
With my shore , I've formed a bond .

- Manogyna Podila

Meanings :

1. Bond - a relationship.
2. Cozy - giving a feeling of comfort, warmth, and relaxation.

49. Only You

I thought you were hard to me ,
I thought you were rude to me ;
I thought you were bad to me ,
I am of course a lad to thee .
I used to never help you ,
I used to never care for you ;
I used to never listen to you ,
But I was never a burden to you .
I said , leave my home I will ,
I said , move away I will ;
I said , neither talk I will ,
Now , I remember those words that kill .
Atlast , I need some good ,
Atlast , I need my blood ;
Atlast , I need that few ,
Atlast , I need only you .
Now , I can understand the pain ,
And am unable to live away ;
With your memories , I go through ,
Mom and Dad , I love you !

- Manogyna Podila

Meanings :

1. *Lad - a child.*
2. *Thee - you.*

50. Wild Friends Wild Dreams

Wild friends, wild friends here and there,
wild friends, wild friends everywhere!
You and me both are wild friends,
joining the wild trends!
You and me everlasting bonds...
Clicking a photograph is it much fun?
near the bunds,
isn't this idea known by none?
The time the teacher said "say cheese"
everyone went like 'geez'...
It is much funny when we click with these.
I love my friends though they're wild,
I like my friends and make them mild;
But never mind being a child...
They come in dreams ,
shining like beams;
Making me laugh...
with cruel gleams!

- Manogyna Podila

Meanings :

1. *Trends - a general change or development.*
2. *Bunds - an artificial embankment.*
3. *Mild - not very bad.*
4. *Beams - light.*
5. *Geez - The word geez is an informal way to express surprise, disappointment, frustration, annoyance, or exasperation.*
6. *Gleams - a sudden expression of emotion in somebody's eyes.*

51. Beach

"Oh have a look at that beach"
said the voice beside;
"Just stop it, you lazy preach"
said the voice aside.
"Don't you like this scenery?"
shouted a girl afar;
"You're silly, admiring greenery"
pointed a boy before.
"How beautiful is the nature"
cried a man beyond;
"I hate the nature and its feature"
whispered a woman annoyed.
"Hey! please stop this nonsense"
exclaimed a pretty little child;
"You all seem to wear the lens"
that's what makes you mild.
"Girl and boy and man and woman"
try just to beautify the beach;
"No one's ready to share the fun"
rather than sit in bleach.

- Manogyna Podila

52. Savitribai Phule

She was a teacher and a poet,
who fought for girls' right and equality;
Along with her husband, Jyotirao Phule,
she faced bravely every difficulty.
She is known as the mother of indian feminism,
she always had in her heart, the feeling of optimism.
She worked to abolish,
discrimination based on caste and gender;
Savitribai Phule is a lady,
who never surrendered.
To educate girl child,
was her main objective and aim;
Through hard-work and tolerance,
she earned her fame.
She taught the nation, girls' right by,
becoming the first lady teacher;
And she inspires us to achieve our dreams,
with wisdom and courage it seems.
As our future the brighest we make,
By following the path that leads to success for our sake!

- Manogyna Podila

Meanings :

1. *Feminism - the belief that woman should have the same rights and opportunities as men.*
2. *Optimism - the feeling that the future will be good or successful.*
3. *Discrimintion - treating one person or one group worse than others.*
4. *Objective - something that you are trying to achieve.*
5. *Aim - a purpose.*
6. *Tolerance - capacity to endure pain and hardhsips.*
7. *Fame - being known or talked about a person or many people because of what you have achieved.*

53. My Preacher

Once, I heard about feature
and immediately asked the teacher
whom, I thought the best creature
will be my so loved preacher.
My teacher was so cool
and lent me an old tool
I thought she was making me fool
but inside that was some wool.
My mind got upset
would speak completely and will bet
only when me, she would let.
Then too much happy, I be
if she responded to me so free
but it would be a dream, I see
not at all posibble with she.
How, the world bears this torture?
only just for knowing this feature
then comes in mind arriving future
only reasoned because of preacher.
Why curse my teacher ahead?
all like me, up they fed
no one likes to care such dead

the only option left...
is to sleep on bed!

- Manogyna Podila

54. Michelle Obama

As first lady of United States,
Michelle Obama loved her team-mates.
Served as a role model for women,
she was considered as a fashion icon.
Born as Michelle Robinson,
grew up with the fame as Mrs. Obama;
Is lawyer, wrtier, designer and more,
loves to work which would never bore.
Mother of Malia and Shasha,
daughter of Marian and Fraser;
Wife of the great Barack Obama,
she's the best inspiration to you and me.
And never gave up;
until she'd succeed...!

- Manogyna Podila

Meanings :

1. *Fame - the state of being known or talked about by many*
   people, especially on account of notable achievements.

55. It's Life

For the good and bad,
for the better and worse;
for the best and worst...
It's life, we are living and made to live,
it's pure to know what you have and give.
Just focusing on what we're made all here,
there is the need to sit and clear.
Gather around and make world know,
the reason for you;
until you always go.
Making efforts for your goals right now,
will make you a star, when all before you bow.
So take it easy, all my friends!
and start your day with new life trends.
Make the world brighter,
as long as you live;
Let your future,
to give-give-give!

- Manogyna Podila

56. My Tata

It's been long since I saw him,
its being true for me and him;
I am sure I will meet him,
with the end of getting spring.
The way he taught me things so far,
the way he made me good;
fed me basic need of living life,
and gave importance to the ones' so should.
He used to pamper me when young,
and now also too...
would ofter watch movies late at night,
both horror and terrifying too.
He poured knowledge a lot,
on things mysterious to say;
he always cared for all,
a happy life for him, I pray.
He's no. 1 for me,
my grandpa's always cool;
for all the ones I say,
I love my grandpa much too!

- Manogyna Podila

Meanings :

1. *Terrifying - causing extreme fear.*

57. Noon

Once upon a time
I went bla-bla-bla,
all the day with chores
it meant shaka-laka.
There was hardly someone
who had my blows,
but never they did spend
with me without being forced.
Still in hunger begging for to jump,
if I had a chance to run-run-run.
Somebody to chase me
along my way,
i'd be happy
to share my day.
But all in vain, for me I say,
for in time fear, as I move gay.

- Manogyna Podila

58. Helling Goal

I thought to be a teacher
at the age of five,
when I saw my teacher
shouting at us, although we were fine.
I thought to be a doctor
at the age of eight,
when I saw my people
crying helplessly for fate.
I thought to be a professor
at the age of twelve,
when I saw the silly lecturers
working alone for themselves.
I'm thinking of being a business person
at my teen right now,
would you suggest something good
then to you, I sincerely bow.
I think farming would be the best
for mind and body and soul,
I am pretty fed up
in looking for the helling goal.

- Manogyna Podila

Meanings :

1. *Fate - the development of events outside a person's control, regarded as predetermined by a supernatural power.*
2. *Helling - disgust or impatience.*

59. Thoughts

Those hide in a big pot,
and burst out at once;
fly along my way,
before getting tons and tons.
I do not know what to do,
I think off, I think off;
at last I get my mind,
under control before bursting out.
My day passes by,
still I focus on;
no clarity but words mix up,
finally I note them down!

- Manogyna Podila

Meanings :

1. Tons - immense.

60. Dejection

You were good to me at first
were taking care of mine,
would make me happy all the while
and everything was fine.
The present days have changed
atlast you ignore me now,
and forget me at once
to your loyalty I bow.
You left me alone
I felt heartbroken,
there was all pain
since you've spoken.
My little world is empty
without you in my rife,
though it feels a bit bad
I wish you to enjoy your life.
You didn't mind it good
there were many options to go,
I thought I was dying
when I was left in a pool of sorrow.
You hurt me so far
I remember those days you've gove,

we had fun together
and this is my masterpiece of love.
Still there are moments good
which I can survive hard,
even you are away
you're always in my heart.
I give away my hopes
whatever you showed was fake,
it is already late
now it's time for break.

- Manogyna Podila

Meanings :

1. *Gove - stare.*
2. *Rife - common occurence, widespread.*

61. Pluto Case

Mom , what if he were so big ?
He's just four big than me ;
You're pampering him a lot so far ,
And he's more than me for thee .
He doesn't help you , neither he studies
He's your world and all ;
And I here , am nothing to you ,
Though I run and come , when you call .
You give him money , but not to me
You send him out , but never me ;
You gifted him a cycle , and not to me
You laugh with him , but always scold me .
Mom , am I very bad to you ,
Or what if he's a prince ;
Then am I not a princess to you ,
I'm being hurt a lot since .
If I ask you , you say ,
I am a gem and I'd to be kept safe ;
Then what about your elder stone ,
Is it a Pluto case ?

- Manogyna Podila

Meanings :

1. *Pampering - to treat with extreme or excessive care and attention.*

62. Gardyloo

Kangaroo can jump, I can walk;
wait a second, there's more to talk.
Fish can swim, I can feel;
they had a trim, and I had a heel.
Breeze blows hard, little mood swings;
I go mad, my memory sinks.
The tree stand stood, I can see;
he does he could, but still not free.
Weather grew cold, it started to rain;
I felt bold, and felt no pain.
A fresh chick came, and wandered around;
it felt no harm, so it moved along.
By the grace of god, all is good;
things got wierd, they could not so should.
The fate is at play, it made its mind;
not everyone can bear, only a mother could withstand.

- Manogyna Podila

Meanings :

1.   *Gardyloo - a warning cry.*

63. No One Elsewhere

In a bane of flood ,
Affright of the buck ;
That fervent circumjacent …
Neither with the couch ,

Nor the flipping fire ;
Mother let me go ,
To the present …
The garth of a whim ,
Indeed a freeze o'er oath ;
With a halt and lame of a heaven …
It's a shatter of a grief ,
The laud of a knafe ;
The hinder of a man ,
And a curse of a slave …
In spite of a lier ,
Who extols me the power ;
Maybe I do linger ,
With no one elsewhere !

- Manogyna Podila

Meanings :

1. *Bane - poison.*
2. *Affright - frighten of.*
3. *Buck - a daring young man.*
4. *Fervent - hot or glowing.*
5. *Circumjacent - surrounding.*
6. *Garth - an open space.*
7. *Whim - a sudden desire or change of mind, especially one that is unusual or unexplained.*
8. *O'er - over.*
9. *Laud - praise.*
10. *Knave - a dishonest or unscrupulous man.*
11. *Hinder - make it harder for someone.*
12. *Extols - praise or give away enthusiastically.*
13. *Linger - spend long time over travelling.*

64. Love

Love belongs to everyone who really needs it,
love is acquired by the people those fit.
Love between a girl and girl is always very caring,
love bestowed to those two , is admiringly sharing.
Love between a boy and boy is rather either related,
love bestowed to those two, is ever never faded.
Love between a boy and a girl is the relation unknown,
love bestowed to those two, is protected from lone.
Love is a mystery which opened people's minds,
love changed the berk to the heavenly kinds.
Love is so simple as caught to many,
love is not like pimple to have done deny.
Love is so pleasant which denotes togetherness,
love is nothing but bringing happiness.

- Manogyna Podila

65. The Big-Pocket

Steps go wide,
over peny over penny;
Disastrous they be,
neither silly nor funny.
Thinking of the next,
meseems curious little lady;
afraid of the beast,
belike sick and shady.
A buss in a temper,
a glim over charm;
A reward for the grateful,
an orison to the psalm.
With a horseless carriage,
heyday be the way;
For messing up the means,
enjoy as they lay!

- Manogyna Podila

Meanings :

1. *Meseems - it seems to me.*
2. *Buss - a kiss.*
3. *Glim - a candle or lantern.*

4.   *Orison - a prayer.*
5.   *Psalm - a sacred hymn.*
6.   *Messing - making untidy or dirty.*

66. Traffic Jam

At the world what a pity,
for the means I am hurry;
By the living restless throng,
I do think who I am.
Deserted in the morning,
feeling lame dark at night;
dreadful be the beasts,
all alone ever at sight.
With horns and the grumbling,
streets they too bound;
With lights and mazes,
for the heavenly found.
For all the hopes and patience,
we hold, when held in a traffic jam.

- Manogyna Podila

Meanings :

1. *Throng - a large, densely packed crowd of people or animals.*
2. *Deserted - empty of people.*
3. *Lame - uninspiring or dull.*
4. *Grumbling - expressing a complaint in a bad-tempered way.*
5. *Maze - a confusing intricate network of passages.*

67. Big Hit

Am last in the party
they drank alone at night
Maybe for my father
I jumped my wall off sight.
Oh! that was nice
again i'd to do, again-again
it was dark by the road caught up.
My mom stood aright
back then I could remember
for my mother, I fought
the song, I do listen to.
My mouth watering up
Oh! the clouds that wish me
passage drawn above my lite
the then, I hook upon thee.
For the soul that i'm free
my god it pains, as on showers
yeah please let me,
give it too thee...!!

- Manogyna Podila

68. Colours

The sky is blue, it away flew;
the grass is green, i'm so keen.
The pot is pink, containing ink;
the flowers are red, the flower bed.
The boat is brown, it roamed the town;
the hat is yellow, it caught that fellow.
The shoes are orange, I found a sporange;
the room is black, I thought to sack.
The people are white, they're flying kite;
the kite is purple, it made a burble.
The fruit is violet, that assured the pilot;
we are all beige, mostly sage.
The hair is gray, the donkey does bray;
the frock is cyan, it had a time span.
The bird is magenta, then occured tormenta;
the watch is golden, my voice bolden.
The plate is silver, I saw a chilver;
The shop is argent, that's the margent.

- Manogyna Podila

Meanings :

1. Keen - eager and enthusiastic.

2. *Sporange - a single-celled or many-celled structure in which spores produced especially in fungi, algae, mosses and ferns.*

3. *Sack - (in the past) attack, steal from, and destroyed a place.*

4. *Burble - make continuous murmuring sound.*

5. *Beige - shades of skin colour.*

6. *Sage - wise.*

7. *Cyan - greenish-blue colour.*

8. *Span - lasts or continuous for a particular period of time.*

9. *Tormenta - storm.*

10. *Bolden - to take courage.*

11. *Chilver - a newborn young female lamb.*

12. *Argent - silvery white colour.*

13. *Margent - a margin, border or edge.*

69. It's Me

When I asked him to tell the truth
he made many a gestures,
but after being asked the same again
he made use of different features.
I was irritated a lot alone
though much earlier, i've replied to the same,
not that hard, i'd thought after
for it's only the truth and dare game.
He was feeling shy to state
as it's difficult not the easy at last,
he pretended to think for long, I say
as always the question was wide and vast.
He led me wait, for I took four days
simply praying for answer in ways,
i'd not left him but begged for clue
at last he said that, "it is you!"

- Manogyna Podila
To my Cute little Brother ARUN !!

70. A Haunted house

There was a house
Far away my one's,
Which was haunted
by ghosts, devils, spirits and some.
Breeze blows at night,
Foxes howl and fight;
No vehicles pass by nor ways,
No people are visible nor bays.
There's a large burial ground around,
from where we can find some sound;
No one dares to step inside,
They just check whether they return outside.

- Manogyna Podila

Meanings :

1. *Bays - a broad inlet of the sea where the land curves inwards.*

71. Morning

Up came the sun
down the hill it flowed,
high rised the voice
slightly the peacock bowed.
Cool meant the room
When, I laid on the bed,
entered the room, my mom
and that's what she said.
Late's the time running
know what you need,
aim high at the sky
nothing more to feed .
Green looked the grass
there gazed the cow,
the music that's been played
morning's what I love.
Hard rang the bell
hurried me, mother more,
left soon the bus
for me to complete my chore.

- Manogyna Podila

72. Fear

Burst out fear off your mind,
give up fear in the path you find.
Burn your fear for you are right,
let out fear as you may fight.
Blame that fear which leads too bad,
step out of fear as you may turn mad.
Wear out fear that causes you to fail,
spit out fight and move on brave.
When there's fear in your life,
you have to worry for children and wife.
When there's bravery at your toes,
you might carry everything on elbows.

- Manogyna Podila

73. Evening

Down rose the sun,
below the clouds it danced;
merry went by the road,
happily the baby glanced.
Here, the parrot squeked,
there, the street dog barked;
for the heavenly rains,
above the endless sky.
The girl came to mom,
upset, the child, she claimed;
mom shot so quick,
reasoned not I, girl blamed.
Brittle laughed the mom,
caught the baby, hand;
shooked the milk at once,
gave the little infant!

- Manogyna Podila

74. It Is You

Without you, I am not there,
you and me, make a wonderful pair;
thee leave me alone and that's not fair,
to thy, I do so much care.
When you touch my tongue always,
my heart beats hard, for you I praise,
I love you literally as I say;
the way you connect to me and stay,
feel to be with you all day;
to me you're nothing but fey.
I do for you, all day fight,
for you are kept far off my sight.
Lifelorn I be leaving yo
i'm addicted to you and that's so true.
My 'boost', you boost my mind,
and help me live the life I find.
Without you i'll be nowhere, it seem,
to you my life, entirely I deem...
At last I like to say that,
"BOOST IS THE SECRET OF MY ENERGY!"

- Manogyna Podila

Meanings :

1. *Thee - you.*
2. *Thy - your.*
3. *Deem - regard or consider in a specified way.*

75. Does It Happen

Does the earth rotate carrying us?
Does the sun revolve?
Does the bee also buzz?
Does the ripe fruit fall?
Does the God above really exist?
Does the brown bird fly?
Does the air carry the mist?
Does the monkey eat a guy?
Does the fish loves to be dry?
Does the tree age so small?
Does the wound make us cry?
Does the butterfly crawl?
Does it happen?
Asked a little boy standing beside
I didn't knew what to say
shall speak something or shall hide?
Rather than speaking non-sense
i'd told the boy to cross the fence
i've also thought to speak ahead
and pointed out that,
as true as it is true, you live
It does happen sometimes true

to you, without a head.

- Manogyna Podila

76. World Has To Bear It

The phenomenon which occurs most of the time,
not only for this purpose, but to eat the lime;
The world has to bear it, yet for many,
let others think, what they think so funny.
Big to small, love the way we go,
desire too curious, what the world thinks know.
See as something needed special
to the others or you,
for nothing is very important
as to wear a pair of shoe.
World has to bear it, for the lives they live,
let the others decide, to take or to give.
Being the one to soothe the evil, so far,
for the mistakes done on road, but they roam by car.
World has to bear it, as they turn on to head,
let the others be, for what they simply fed.

- Manogyna Podila

Meanings :

1. *Phenomenon - a fact or situation that is observed to exist or happen.*
2. *Soothe - gently calm.*

77. Online Classes

Mute your mics shouts the teacher ahead,
silly kids, you get up from bed;
don't wash your face neither eat your bread,
get up sleepily, to eat my head.
God only knows what to do with you,
who act over smart, so true.
Nor study hard, by everyone you shed,
either dream up good, for all you fed.
Seem to all you clever, once,
but very soon, everyone shuns.
As teacher asks you a question,
you click leave option;
and think to meet on other occasion.
Online classes once ago would seem good,
ask a child if there's a thing she's understood!

- Manogyna Podila

Meanings :

1. Shun - avoid, ignore.

78. Luck

For a word, I waited so long,
he told me to dance or sing a song.
That was quite funny, was I thought,
nothing to do, but sat and fought.
That was interesting for me and him,
we chatted so far by the dark and dim.
I just love to pass time with him,
for he is just my everlasting new sim.
I enjoy each and every moment by side,
I love to talk and sometimes hide.
He never keeps boring, but always good,
he makes me happy as far as he could.
That's my luck, I think i'm lucky,
for there is one, who makes me happy.
He never laughs, but makes me laugh too,
whenever possible, i'd say "I love you!"

- Manogyna Podila

To my Sweet little Brother HANUMAN !!

79. Nature

We can't believe people close to us,
we can't believe people around us.
My hope led to belief,
belief led to hope.
Sunshine gave me faith,
and all the strength to cope.
My pain led me strong,
strength led to courage;
trees gave me confidence,
and all the way to troops.
My dream led my way,
my path showed the good;
all the things to say,
is to find, what you should.

- Manogyna Podila

Meanings :

1. *Cope - to deal with.*

80. Someone Good

As we all grow,

about the world we know.

Around the cunning and cruel,

we are burning like fuel.

No care for one and all these days,

no love upon the needy and greedy in ways.

Besides peace and harmony, we choose violence,

ruthless people had lost their sense.

No happiness in our lives, we live,

we don't take it, and never give.

Selfish people think all about themselves,

foolish creatures make others their slaves.

Not kind, nor helping, not there in needs,

not polite, nor humble, at last no deeds.

All are jealous, there's no grace,

in life troubles, we all will face.

All are rude and rough,

how this life's being tough.

Not a person who shares his food,

so in search of someone good.

- Manogyna Podila

81. Taking Leave

After the years of labour service,
after the tears of sweat;
after the work on knees,
after the pains of regret.
It's time to explore the world,
and learn much from nature;
time to live for myself and old,
and observe every creature.
The hardwork which led the person at height,
gives happiness by the step and side;
keeps experiencing the evil and might,
let us soon span the tide.
It's time to pay the life abroad,
all the knowledge to give;
beyond the clouds, in search of God,
At last, i'm taking leave.

- Manogyna Podila

82. Politics

The meaning of politics thereby mean,
governing a country or an area;
But not the thing which is seen,
in present days of Asia.
Politics is not made to fulfil one's stomachs,
all politicians are rather than greedy lying berks;
the politics which is being observed,
is fully being polluted.
They mostly think that they have served,
and in them selfishness diluted.
The country they are working for,
is meant for their own satisfaction;
but before elections, they prove sure,
not very later, they turn faction.
This is the time to polish,
the one's in the politics who seem foolish;
with dedication, if they seem right,
that's the politics perfect.

- Manogyna Podila

Meanings :

1.   Berks - a stupid or foolish person.

83. Old

Old is gold, old is bold,
old is true, old is blue.
Old is pure, old is cure,
old is light, old is bright.
Old is love, old is above,
old is care, old is share.
Old is life, old is rife,
old is free, old is glee.
Old is a period of our life,
when we have both children and wife.
Old is a period when we're weak,
and the help we have to seek.
Old is inspiration to the young,
when we get wrinkles from toes to tongue.
Old is something not so new,
old are everyone and not that few.

- Manogyna Podila

84. Last Breadth

Left the home and the living,
left the caring and the loving;
Left the family and the friends,
left the memories and the trends;
Left the little and the old,
left the weak and the bold;
Left every, one and all,
left by God's call;
Left us depressed alone,
left sorrow and lone;
Left to heaven above,
left us all by love;
Left overcoming everyone's need,
left the life's greed;
Left us in grief,
left the last leaf;
Left behind old month,
left the last breadth.

- Manogyna Podila

Meanings :

1. *Depression - feelings of severe despondency and dejection.*

85. Marriage Anniversary

Sweet moments of happiness and care,
your love for others, you should share!
We see youngsters growing old,
and also notice elders standing bold;
Please have patience to scold,
but in your minds, you should hold.
Wishing a happy married life;
to the both, husband and wife!
Give out misery you've gained,
forget the hardships you've pained;
for that never should be shamed,
always, as you, me tamed.
Ever you two keep signing high,
never you should feel bit shy;
for all, you are a lovely guy,
no! I like to say bye-bye.
Have a look at each other once,
without even using the lens;
can eat after, many times buns,
enjoy the life that brings you funs'.
Be the one expelling light,
forever seem everytime bright;

anywhere if I just caught a sight,
I will kiss you, that be might.
Wishing a happy married life;
to the both, husband and wife!

- Manogyna Podila

Meanings :

1.   *Expelling - force out (something), especially from the body.*

86. Birth and Death

We are born to live the world,
we are died to leave the world
We are made to make the world,
we are designed to journey the world.
We are signed to rule the world,
we are layed to present the world.
We are caused to develop the world,
we are shaped to discover the world.
We are sealed to soothe the world,
we are here to vitalize the world.
Life is full of gifts I know, but think about the one's I say,
they are birth and death we live about and simply do we play.
Life is the one which nowadays turned vitiate,
birth and death are the accidents which everyone always hate.
These two are the presents which resign only once,
so take them into account happily as you do to the tons.

- Manogyna Podila

Meanings :

1. *Vitalize - give strenth and energy to.*
2. *Vitiate - make less good or effective.*
3. *Soothe - calm.*

4. *Resign - accept that something bad and undesirable cannot be avoided.*

5. *Ton - large number.*

87. Silly Mistakes

Here mark gone, there mark gone
and you name them silly,
this is because, you weren't fawn
but your mind was on the rose and lilly.
Mistakes are mistakes
though you make them silly,
this is your fault
as you're not taking any.
Be little careful, for I do say,
not to be like grasshopper, for he lives gay.
You are the subject
where you have to point,
not the other catch your object
for them, they seem gaint.
So do not make mistakes
following the name silly,
as your mind will be on the rose and lilly.

- Manogyna Podila

88. Our Tiny-tot

She's so cute

she's so sweet

she's so lovely...

She's so brilliant

she's so beautiful

she's so awesome...

She's like doraemon

her hairs like rapunzel

moreover a tiny-tot!

Her spects are glooming...

her scent is gleaming

her shoes are dancing...

her cheeks are singing

her saree is swinging

her maths is dreaming...

Dare to say that her eyes are always

peeping right into our hearts...!

Never punishing, always securing

She's none other than our tiny-tot

great... miss

- Manogyna Podila

Meanings :

1. *Awesome - impressive.*
2. *Glooming - dark.*
3. *Gleaming - shining.*
4. *Securing - to make something safe.*

89. A Best Partner

- Manogyna Podila

Meanings :

1.   *Glance - a quick look.*

90. Competing with Corona

There was a time when restless people,
were falling at doors;
when some them were isolated,
and some of them busy at chores.
The virus was spreading rapidly,
among the streets and stores;
but not all was strict and not all was forced.
It was named Corona, all the epidemic wide,
while creatures some, not able to fight;
layed their lives aside.
Some thought it's fatal, others named it cool,
other some day, they proved to be a fool.
It conveyed the fellow beings that,
not the size which matters hard;
by the craze that chased so far,
all big to small and rich to poor.
Age is just a number,
we should ever remember;
when comes in the point of view to life,
it's same for the begging and also for the giving.

- Manogyna Podila

91. धरती पुत्र

बुरी बुरी है बात वो,
आई मेरी ख़याल में,
सुना समझने की कोशिश है,
मेरे दिल को प्यार से
भटकगया है मन मेरा,
आराम की आवश्यकता है।
सामान्यों का जीवन है,
कठिनाईयों से भरा है,
पार करना मुश्किल है
हाथ हमारे नहीं है
देख रहा है जीवन है
लेकिन हिम्मत नहीं हम तोड़ते है
गरीब है तो होने दो,
ज़मीन पर हम बसते है
एक बार पंछी खोले,
ऊँचे आसमान में उड़ जाते है
जीवन हमारा सरल है,
ताकत हमारी तेज़ी है
आसानी से हार न मानते,
भारत माँ को मन से पुकारते

मटिटी के साथ बढ़े हम बच्चे,
खुले हवा में खेले खूदे,
पेट काँटकर खेती करते;
हम धरती के पुत्र कहलातो

- मनोज्ञा पोदलिा

92. मेरी गुड़िया

बनाई मैंने गुड़िया छोटी छोटी बाल वाली,
अनुमति के बिना, अंजान के हाथ में न डाली।
देख देखी वह मेरी बच्ची सुंदर और सुहानी,
इस्तमाल मैंने कयिा बनाने कपड़े बहुत पुरानी।
सजाई मैंने कुंदन से, उसे खूब सुंदर कहलायी,
रात को हाथ लेकर, पास अपने सुलाई।
साथ और साथ, खेली खूदी खाई और मुस्कुराई,
बातो ंबात बोली बच्ची प्यारी और न्यारी।
बड़ी भोली मेरी बच्ची मदद खूब कर आई,
अपने तेज़ बड़े आखो ंसे घर पूरा मँडरायी।
खून पसीना इकट्ठा कर, पैसे बेगे बचाके लाई,
आखरि वह छोटी गुड़िया, मैंने खुद बनाई!

- मनोज्आ पोदलिा

93. कोरोना

महामारी फैलि निकिला २०१९ में,
नाम रखा गया कोरोना।
घर अपना बना लिया विश्व में,
बात हुई तब, 'क्या है कोरोना?'
सरकार ने किया फरियाद,
बोला वैक्सीन बनाओ;
नहीं तो दुनिया बरबाद।
घर से बाहर निकिलना नहीं,
क्या नहीं जी सकते बिना दूध और दही?
बिल्कुल नहीं छोड़ना है घर,
बैठो अंदर पूरा दिन भर।
अगर लड़ना है कोरोना से,
फैलि दूर करो अंधविश्वास सबको
प्राण निकिल जाते है अभी,
भगाओ उसको, नहीं आए कभी।
दूर रहो एक दूसरे के साथ,
नहीं मिलाना बिल्कुल हाथ।
हाथ-पाँव अक्सर से धोना,
बात तुम मानो और खुश जीना।
इम्युनिटी है अब बढ़ाना,

धूप का महत्त्व नहीं जनता यह जमाना।

प्राण से मुख्य हैं कुछ नहीं,
सरकार ने बोला वो सब सही।

आगा तुम कोरोना से फिर लड़ते,

फिर ही बचते, नहीं तो मरतो

- मनोज्ञा पोदिला

94. लोखड़ौन

लोखड़ौन की करो बात,
तो क्या बोलू ज़िंदगी बरबाद।
एक तरफ अच्छी ही वो,
दूसरी तरफ होता है बोर।
दिन और रात बैठे है अंदर,
नहीं है आलू टमाटर, सकिंदर।
किराना का तो है ही हाल,
हस्ते रहो साबून से काल।
पानी में डालो, तीन घंटे सही,
नमक का डालना भूलना ही नहीं।
आदमी का आकर है देखो,
कसरत घर में करते ही सीखो।
ऑनलाइन का यह नया जमाना,
होता है अब वह फिर पुराना।
एक ओर कोरोना से लड़ते,
दूसरी ओर हाथ-पैर ही धोते।
यह बोलो स्थिति भयंकर,
जय राम-सीता, हो! शिव-शंकर।
है भाई, ए.सी. में न बैठो,
उसके आलावा ज़मीन पर लेठो।

मोदी जी का बात जब मानो,
यह पूरा विश्वास मन में ठानो।

- मनोज्ञा पोदिला

95. आई मेरी आई

आई-आई मेरी आई,
आई मेरी आई।
बहुत प्यारी मेरी आई,
आई मेरी आई।
सुनी समझायी मेरी आई,
प्यार से खूप मुसुकुराई।
आई मेरी आई !
डाँट कभी न खाना,
मार कभी न खाना।
बात कभी भी सुनलेना,
बस बचना उससे हाई।
मस्ती खूप करना,
पूरा दिन खेलना;
पढ़ाई न करना,
तो आई मेरी आई।
आई-आई मेरी आई,
आई मेरी आई !

- मनोज्ञा पोदलिा

96. दोस्त

दोस्त होते हैं अच्छे,
और कभी कभी कच्चे
सुन लेना उनकी बात,
परंतु हो जाना बरबाद।
प्यार हमें वो करते,
सँभालते हमें अच्छे से
कभी होते हैं कट्टी,
फिर पूरा दिन छुट्टी।
झगड़ना मत,
परंतु दोस्ती बढ़ाना।
तब होती है कमरी कुट्टी।
मित्र बढ़ाना,
उनकी दोस्ती बढ़ाना।
फिर होगी हमारी दिन खुशी-खुशी !

- मनोज्ञा पोदलिा

97. जंगल

होता है जंगल बड़ा विशाल,

कहलाता है जंगल प्राणियों और पक्षियों का घर।

भर जाता है जंगल पेड़ों और फलों से,

जानवरों और पक्षियों से

हान मत पहुँचाना जंगलों को,

तब वह खुद हमें हानि पहुँचाते हो

पेड़ हमें ऑक्सीजन देते हैं,

जो हमें जीने के लिए आवश्यक हो

पेड़ मत काटना,

उसके जगह;

भरपूर पौधे नाटँना।

- मनोज्ञा पोदलि

98. रीसेस

मी आणली बाटल्या,
बाटल्या सोबत दब्या !
दब्यात होता नान,
खायला खूप छान-छान !
माझ्या जवळ आहे भरपूर,
ऊद्या घेणार दब्यात अंकुर !
रीसे झाली सुरु
पोट पूरण भरु !
पोटात घेला खाऊ,
पण अजून पाहिजे काय घेऊ ?
बाटल्यात भरली पाणी,
इतक्यात नको शहाणी !
पाऊस आली सर-सर,
मी भगायला गेली घर-घर !
ऊन-सावली म्हणून काय,
माई बनवात दररोज शविाय !
रोटी, पूरी, दाल, वडा,
इडली साठी नही वंडा !
बोला कसे बनवत खाऊला,
धन्यवाद करत माझे आईला !

- *मनोज्ञा पोदलि*

99. शक्षिक दविस

मानत हैं हम शक्षिक दविस ५ सतिंबंर को,
प्रणाम करत हैं उन महँ को चलो।
अर्थ बताता हैं शक्षिक, शक्षिा दने वाला,
हम सही और गलत का रास्ता दखिन वाला।
हमार अंध्कार को शक्षिक, ज्ञान के प्रकाश से हमेशा के लिए दूर
करत हैं,
वही हमारा मार्गदर्शन कर, हमार भवष्यि का नर्मिाण करत हौ
गुरु ही ब्रह्मा, गुरु ही वष्णिु, गुरु ही दवे, गुरु ही महेश्वर,
आशीर्वाद प्राप्त करत हैं, उन्ह वंदन कर।
तो चल मानत डॉ सर्वपल्ली राधाकृष्णन के नाम प शक्षिक
दविस,
हे वज्ञिान ! शक्षिको कं रूप स हमेशा बरस।
" सब धरती कागज करुं लखिनी सब बनराय।
सात समुन्दर की मसकिरुं गुरु गुण लखिा न जाय।"

- मनोज्ञा पोदलिा

100. शब्द संपदा

शब्द ही विचित्र है,
शब्द ही स्वाभाविक है;
शब्द ही अपूर्व है,
शब्द ही स्वरूप हौ
शब्दों से अक्षर,
अक्षर से वाक्य;
वाक्य से महावाक्य।
महावाक्य से पाठ,
पाठ से किताब;
किताब से ग्रन्थ।
शब्द ह इस दुनिया में भरे हौं
शब्दों का अर्थ जानो,
शब्दों का अर्थ बनाओ;
शब्दों का अर्थ बताओ,
शब्दों की महत्त्व सिखाओ।

- मनोज्ञा पोदिला

Thanking you

~ the author